Also available from Central Avenue Publishing
in the I Wrote This For You Series:

I Wrote This For You
*The first collection of photography and prose
from I Wrote This For You.*

I Wrote This For You: Just The Words
*An expanded collection of the prose
from I Wrote This For You.*

I WROTE THIS FOR YOU

AND ONLY YOU

pleasefindthis

central
avenue
publishing

2015

Central Avenue Publishing Edition

Copyright © 2015 Central Avenue Publishing

All rights reserved. No part of this book may be used or reproduced in any manner whatsoever without written permission from the author and photographer except in the case of brief quotations embodied in critical articles and reviews.

This edition is published by arrangement with the author and photographer, contact at pleasefindthis@gmail.com

Central Avenue Publishing - www.centralavenuepublishing.com

First printing published by Central Avenue Publishing, a division of Central Avenue Marketing Ltd.

I WROTE THIS FOR YOU AND ONLY YOU

ISBN 978-1-77168-042-4 (pbk)
ISBN 978-1-77168-028-8 (ebk)

1. POETRY / Subjects & Themes - General   2. PHOTOGRAPHY / Subjects & Themes - General

Published in Canada. Printed in the United States of America.

Dear You,

Thank you for finding this book, I assure you it has been lost, and looking for you, for far too long.

As you hold it now, is how I held it before it left my hands.

All I'm trying to say still echoes through these pages.

Thank you for reading and for hearing.

Wherever this finds you, I hope it finds you well.

- Me

THE STARS LOOK LIKE DROPS OF WHITE PAINT

I know you might think that you're just sitting there, looking at some random book, reading some stupid words and maybe the world has told you who you are for so long that you've started to believe it. But, please, remember that you're so much more than this.

Remember who you really are.

THE TIME YOU NEARLY DIED WHEN YOU WERE STILL OLDER

As you fell, you begged the air for just a little more time, for a second chance to do all the things you'd always meant to do.

So here it is.

You'll remember nothing of what happened.

You'll feel exactly the same.

You'll find yourself back in front of this book, reading the same words on the same page that started it all so many years ago.

And only the words in this sentence have changed.

And this is a little more time.

And this is your second chance.

And it starts: Now.

THE SILVER ASTROLABE

Remember,

There's a map beneath
your skin and all
your veins are rivers,
there's directions and
instructions written in
secret on your bones,
there's a star you
can't see that shines
in a North you'll never
know.

And a secret current,
beneath the waves,
that carries you to the
end of you.

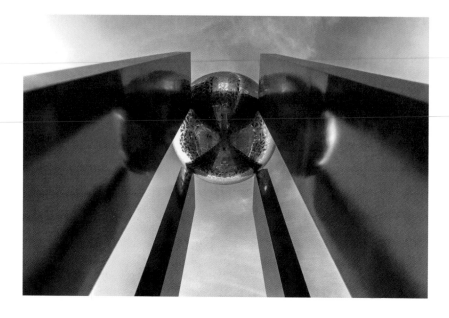

THE ILLUSION OF THINGS NEVER CHANGING

You think, "This is life, this is just how it is and how it'll always be." But you are living through something. And while, logically, you must know that there was a time before now, when things were different, and that there will be a time after now, and things will change, it's so hard to remember right now: Everything will change.

You are alive in a memory.

You, are once upon a time.

THE DREAMS ON THE LINE

I chased my dreams until I caught them.

I chased my thoughts until I stopped thinking.

And I chased my heart until I found you.

THE ANXIETY INHERENT IN AIR

If you must know, this is what I'm scared of. I'm scared that everyone else is more who they are than I am who I am. I think everyone else just looks at the things they feel or think and says, "Of course this is what I feel or think, this is who I am."

But I am never sure of what I feel or think.

And I'm scared because I'm holding all the things I could feel or think on a boat that the slightest breeze could tip over and if that happens, I will fall with all of it into the water. I am scared I will be left with nothing and no idea who I am.

I am scared of the wind.

THE NATURE OF SCIENCE

I have theories about what it takes to talk to you again.

I have theories about what normal is supposed to feel like.

I have theories about how many times a heart can be heard.

Just theories.

THE REMINDER OF THE THING YOU SAID YOU'D DO

Try and remember what you said you'd do and why you said you'd do it.

Forget what you think other people want the thing you said you'd do to be.

The thing you said you'd do should only be what you want the thing you said you'd do to be.

If the thing you said you'd do makes other people happy, that's great but don't say things or do things just to make them happy.

Find new ways to do the thing you said you'd do that don't change the meaning of what you said you'd do.

Have the purest of intentions for what you said you'd do and do it bravely.

If the thing you said you'd do becomes successful, continue to act and think like it is unsuccessful, otherwise you'll spend your time worrying that it might become unsuccessful.

If you said you'd involve people in the thing you said you'd do, listen to them when they say what they think you should do.

If you said you'd do the thing you said you'd do alone, then go boldly into the wilderness and may your own soul be company enough, while you do the thing you said you'd do.

Do right by the thing you said you'd do. Tend to it and love it.

By trying to remember what you said you'd do and the reason why you said you'd do it.

THE REFLECTION IN SHOP WINDOWS

If you live in your head for too long, you run the risk of becoming your own secret.

THE SOFT CRACKLE

Yet love's like a needle on a record, taking parts of you away as it draws sharply and constantly across the heart, in slow descending circles, just to hear a song hidden in the scratches one more time.

THE FELLOW PASSENGER ON A CRASHING TRAIN

Even though I've just met you, I believe we will be friends.

First, I will tell you something about me, then you can tell me something about you, as that, I believe, is how friendship works.

Here is something I believe: I believe that people don't know how people work when they're young and maybe that's why we're so reckless with each other when we're young.

I think people think that people come and go, in and out of life and I think that school teaches them that, that life changes in big annual movements, that one year you're this and the next, you're that. But life blends into itself as you get older and you realise, you will watch a few, if not many, of your friends get old.

You will watch them lose their minds and their hair. You will watch them get sick and get better. You will watch them succeed and fail. You will watch them get married, get divorced, get pregnant and yes, eventually, you will watch them die. Or they will watch you die.

So this is what I believe friendship means. And I'm sorry to have to put such a heavy burden on you. But you have put the same burden on me.

Now you can tell me something you believe, as it is your turn, and this is how friendship works.

THE PICTURES FROM THE CAMERA WE THREW AWAY

Everyone wants to show you pictures of the things you used to do together but all you can do, is wonder why no one's taking new ones.

THE FUTURE IS MADE OF STONES

Don't be angry and make art often. For those of you who do not make art, will make war. And those of you who do not make war, will be left to make art from what remains.

THE WEIGHT OF STONE

If you tie every word you've ever heard about yourself on a string around your head, one day you won't be able to lift it anymore.

THE MAP OF SHADOWS

Sometimes I want to ask complete strangers who have never even met me or had any interaction with me, who have done nothing to influence my experience of the world in any respect whatsoever,

"How can you hate me as much as you do?"

And other days, I know they don't even know me. And maybe they would be ok with me, if they did.

THE COMPLICATIONS START WITH YOU

Here is the simple truth about people: Love the ones you want to keep.

THE OBJECTION YOUR HONOUR

Just then, right in the middle of the brilliant monologue your defence attorney is delivering about all the things you've done and all the people who love you, the prosecution slides a note over to you, "Don't ever forget, everybody hates you."

You add it to the pile of notes he's already given you, which read:

"No one will ever understand you in the way that you desperately want them to understand you."

"You will watch all your favourite musicians kill themselves and all your movie stars will grow old."

"Everything you've ever made has been trite and cliche and horrible. In fact anyone who's ever said they've liked anything of yours has done so out of pity."

"One day you and someone you love will find yourself in a room and one of you will be dead and the other will wish they were."

All of which he will later enter as Exhibit B in the long, drawn out court case to convict you of being simply pathetic and sad and useless at everything, really.

And yet your defence attorney carries on. And you know that sometimes, he's fighting for your life.

THE PROTECTIVE NATURE OF GLASS

I sometimes wonder what you're thinking of me, then I remember that you're probably wondering what I think of you, which makes me wonder if any of us ever think of ourselves.

Or if we think of nothing else.

THE VIEW FROM THE HOSPITAL

If you can't let go, you can't put your heart back in your chest.

THE BRIEFEST RESPITE

If all you do is make something beautiful for someone else, even if it's only for a moment, with a single word or small action, you have done a great service.

Because life can be ugly and frustrating and for so many, it is.

THE OCEANIC FEELINGS

The scariest thing you can think of, is giving up the thing that kills you. The thing you can't live without.

THE JACKET WEATHER

Loneliness is a kind of winter. And you drag me, kicking and screaming, into some kind of bright summer.

THE LOVE LIKE SUNLIGHT

I hope one day you get to love someone like you love breathing air or drinking water. Like they are fundamental to your existence, needed and necessary.

I hope you get to love like gravity loves, like the sun loves the earth.

Like warm sunlight upon soil that makes plants grow.

I hope one day you get to love like that.

THE IRON ON THESE TRACKS

Never stop and never settle but settle down for the one who lets you draw cities on their skin with the tips of your fingers.

Never stop and never settle but settle down for the one who knows that some people were taught to ask for help but never who to ask.

Never stop and never settle but settle down for the one who makes you want to be better.

And settle down.

THE STONES FROM OTHER HOUSES

I wonder if houses miss each other.

I wonder if you can hear them creaking at night, in pain for some other structure they once knew.

A view from a window changed forever by a wrecking ball, a storm or a fire. A place where things used to live.

Why would the universe be so cruel, to build two so close to each other, only to take one away?

And what of the house you build, in the ruins?

THE CITY THAT SLEEPS WHERE THEY FELL

I know you move your fingers when you sleep because I have felt them move and I know I must do the same.

And I must wonder how many times we have unconsciously, in dreams or nightmares, reached for each other's hands and never even known.

THE THINGS I COULD DO

At some point in winter, you'll tell yourself a lie.

You'll say that you aren't as good at anything as you once were.

And even though you know it's a lie, it's hard not to believe yourself, when the only thing you've gotten better at, is telling the time between then and now.

THE BLURRED PALACE

I hope you fail often so that you often have things worth learning.

THE MOMENTS DIRECTLY BEFORE AND AFTER

There are so many moments in life and each one must serve a purpose, to connect us from then, to there. So how couldn't you have known, that this would be one of them?

THE WALLS ARE MADE OF LISTS

I hope one day you meet someone who can write a list of ways you're supposed to feel, and that you like every feeling on that list.

THE MOUTH MOVES BUT NO SOUND COMES OUT

"You know I'm not really here, right?"

"Can I talk to you anyway?"

THE TRAVELLER

I am just the hand you touch when you reach for the air, I am just the nerve signal, moving along the wires in your body, I am just trying to reach your heart to make it beat, one more time.

THE WORLD IS NOT AS DARK AS IT SEEMS

You can't hate everyone. You haven't even met most of them.

THE BLUE BLOOD

You were born royalty to those who made you.

They took their crowns and placed them at your feet.

They swapped their robes for working clothes and went to till the fields.

So that one day, you might take off the crown they'd given you and you might give it to someone, new.

And then go and work the fields.

THE COLDNESS OF STONE

It's not the things you don't want that drag you under.
It's the things you think you want.
Those, are the killers.

THE WORDS THAT LEAVE ON LAST BREATHS

Sometimes I wonder if you've only got a certain number of words and sentences in your head and if you use them all up, you get quiet.

Maybe that's why the young have so much to say, while the old hold what little words they have left so close and so tightly in their hearts.

THE LIGHT AND SHADE

The darkness is hidden from you, only by the light.

THE COLD REFLECTION

Never complain that you haven't been given things to say.

One day the world will destroy itself, and you will drown in the words you didn't think you had.

THE WORLD WHISPERS SONGS SOFTLY

At the end of everything, they'll pull you up and whisper in your ear,

"Could you hear the music?"

And so many of us will have no idea what they mean.

THE AMBASSADOR OF BAD THINGS

When something really, really bad happens to you, people will say to you, "I am sorry," even if they had nothing to do with what happened.

And it's because sometimes things happen that are so bad that what they really mean is, "I am acting as an ambassador and on behalf of everything that must hurt so much right now, I say sorry."

Because sometimes things are so bad, someone just has to say it.

THE HANDS YOU GAVE ME

Everything started when my hands touched yours.

And I've done such sad things with my hands since then and I know you have too.

And I know we'll find light in smaller hands than ours one day soon.

And I hope our hands grow old in each other's.

If not, then why have hands, at all.

THE ANGLE AT WHICH WE ARE ALL JUDGED

If you mean it, say it. If you say it, do it. If you don't, then leave it.

THE HEART OUTGROWS THE CHEST

The further inside you hide the hurt, the more it hurts inside.

All wounds need air to heal.

THE IMAGE REPEATED OVER AND OVER

When you let go, it wasn't a rock falling to the ground.

It was a balloon, rising from a child's hand.

THE REMOVAL OF ME

I know what you feel, when you've got nothing left to feel.

THE PLACE I DO NOT REST

Dress your heart and mind in what you love, fill your eyes with wonder and chase the things that inspire and delight you.

For in you, is where I still live.

THE DESPERATE AND CONFUSED

Even if you write down everything that's ever crossed your heart, there will still come a day when none of your words can explain how you feel.

THE GLARING WHITE BEYOND HEARTBREAK

Beyond heartbreak, lies soulbreak, which is when you cannot spend
time with someone, not because you and them have chosen to part
ways, but because they no longer inhabit the Earth.

THE SPACE BETWEEN THE LAMPS

You drive too slowly down the streets where you once lived but you roll up your windows when you stop at the lights (just in case any of the ghosts try to get in).

THE SAND REMEMBERS WHERE WE STOOD

Say good and true things to the water because it will carry us when we become the dust and the dirt of the world.

Because if the oceans and currents are good to us, we will wash up on the same beach again.

Because it would be good to be with you again.

THE STONES MAKE SAND SLOWLY

If you are lucky, one day you'll get the chance to have your life defined by how much you loved and were loved by someone else.

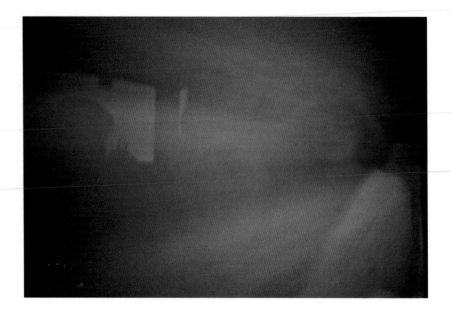

THE MOMENTS YOU HAVE

You are not what you think about doing tomorrow.

You are what you start to do, today.

THE SHAPES LEFT BEHIND

You should not look for me in the places I once was.
Look for me in the places I am now. In soft rain.

On starlit oceans.

THE RIPPLE IN THE CLOUDS

The hardest thing to do when you go back underwater, is talk about what the sky was like.

THE WORLD FALLS AWAY FROM ITSELF

If you promise that you'll save the world, people will believe you.
And when you don't, people will forget what you promised.

THE LANGUAGE BREAKS

You've got such beautiful words but none I can eat, none which block the rain, none which bandage my wounds, none which build a home.

Nothing beautiful, which did not work, ever became anything more than pretty.

THE BOMBS DESTROY MORE THAN JUST CITIES

If you want to make someone cry, make them think of every person who hurt them.

If you want to destroy someone, make them think of every person who they have hurt.

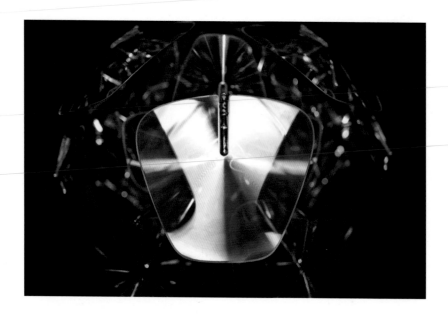

THE NERVE ENDINGS SHATTER LIKE GLASS

It doesn't hurt because if you keep hurting the same part of you again and again and again, the nerve endings all die. And when that happens, that part of you goes numb. That's why it doesn't hurt. Don't be proud of it.

THE ACT OF LIVING IS LETHAL

You forget that even the strongest person to ever live had a weakest day of their life.

THE AGONY OF BEING OTHER PEOPLE

I keep wondering, how many people do you need to be, before you can become yourself.

THE CAMERA IS A BAG FOR MEMORIES

And when someone takes my picture and they tell me to smile, I still think of you.

THE TURNING OF THE SPHERE

"You need to spin the world again."

"Why bother? So what if a few more babies are born. So what if there's heartbreak, pain and pens and doughnuts and washing lines. Who cares if there's forgetfulness and a summer and wine and clouds with faces and shapes hidden in them. That's all that happens every time I spin the world. It's all just a bunch of things that happen. Why bother spinning the world again?"

"Because pens and babies are worth a little heartbreak and pain. Because everyone in the world deserves every chance they can get to find the things and experiences and people that make them happy. So give all of them another chance. Please, spin the world again."

THE NIGHT IS A TUNNEL

I have told the sky all my loneliest thoughts of you. And all it does is shine starlight back at me. But I guess that's what makes it such a good listener.

THE NATURE OF A RIVER IS TO RUN

When it rains, the river will try and take you away from me.

Which is why, when it rains, we must hold onto each other, just a little tighter.

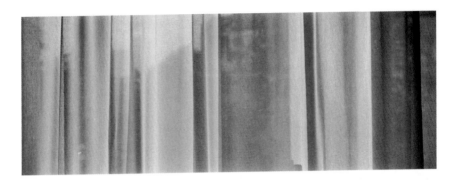

THE SHADOWS ON THE CURTAIN

Sometimes the most important thing you can say is just,

"Are you ok?"

THE TIME KEEPS TWISTING ME

The seconds take a part of me with them. Hopefully to you.

THE THINGS I WOULD'VE SAID

If you're strong enough to take that blade and draw it across your skin.

If you're strong enough to take those pills and swallow them when no one's home.

If you're strong enough to tie that rope and hang it from the ceiling fan.

If you're strong enough to jump off that bridge, my friend.

You are strong enough, to live.

THE SILVER LUMP IN MY THROAT

I hope you know how long it takes me to learn to talk again,
whenever you make me forget.

THE SOUND THAT ENDS THE WORLD

I'm only quiet because I'm worried that if you push me too far, one day I will open my mouth and I will scream so loudly, it will shatter and break the whole world.

THE DIFFERENCE BETWEEN PAINT AND BLOOD

I know you think you define me.

But each brush stroke thinks it's important when it's on the canvas and each brush stroke thinks that it's the last and that the painting will be done when the brush leaves the canvas again.

But it isn't. You are just the shading. You are a dot. And I am the one holding the paintbrush.

THE WORDS ON A TOMBSTONE

Do practical things if you want your tombstone to read,
"They were practical."
Do what makes sense if you think it should say,
"Their life made sense."
Do what the world wants if you believe in the epitaph,
"They did what the world wanted them to do."
But if you want it to read,
"They lived every second they were given
and touched the sky every chance they had,
they burned and blazed in all the colours the eye can see
and left a hole shaped like them in the world
when they left."
Then do something else.

THE PERSON YOU MEET AT THE END IS YOU

The universe curves, as does the Earth. And as hard as you try and run away from everything you are, you'll find yourself where you left yourself when you come home. Just tired.

Fix yourself before you try and outrun yourself.

THE CENTRE OF THE UNIVERSE

"How do you feel?"

"Cold and lonely. Since the beginning of time, everything's been moving away from me. That's what it means to be at the centre. I don't understand why anyone would want to be me."

THE EXPERIENCE BECOMES A STORY

The horror you face today will become the funny story you tell tomorrow.

In the end, everything is overcome and a life is lived.

THE WAY WE'RE MEASURED

You pour yourself into the thing that measures you and it defines you. And I just hope that one day you find out that you're fuller when you measure yourself in love and people and moments, instead of things, adoration and money.

THE EFFICIENCY AND PERFECTION OF THE LOST

Yet you still value the things you've lost the most. Because the things you've lost are still perfect in your head. They never rusted. They never broke. They are made of the memories you once had, which only grow rosier and brighter, day by day. They are made of the dreams of how wonderful things could have been and must never suffer the indignity of actually still existing. Of being real. Of having flaws. Of breaking and deteriorating.

Only the things you no longer have will always be perfect.

THE WINTER CHILD

In bright white snow, when everything sleeps.

And hope has left you lonely.

When all you ever remember about summer is how it ended.

I send hope back to you, wherever you are.

I hope you remember all the people you still have time to be.

I hope the little things in your life inspire you to do big things with it.

I hope you remember that summer comes every year and that the sun, is still sweet.

I hope you learn to hope again.

I, still, hope.

THE STORY CAN NEITHER BE CREATED NOR DESTROYED

As you fall, remember that you are part of a beautiful story that did not start when you were born.

Remember that you are the universe exhaling, a breeze waiting to blow across a field of tall grass.

Remember, you are part of a beautiful story that did not start when you were born.

As your body cuts through the air, think of only the things that made you smile, the people that made you love, the ideas that made you strong.

Remember, those things will never happen again but they cannot unhappen.

Remember, you are part of a beautiful story that did not start when you were born.

Remember, what you felt can't ever be taken away.

Remember, you are part of a beautiful story that did not start when you were born.

And it will not end when you die.

Remember.

THE IMPORTANCE OF CORRECTLY NUMBERING THINGS

There are more grains of sand in the soles of your shoes than you will be given winters to dream or summers to make those dreams real.

And there are more stars in the sky than there are grains of sand on Earth.

We live in a universe so big that a dying star, in the greater scheme of things, is as significant as spilled milk or an unkissed kiss. In an infinite amount of time, everything that can be forgotten, will be forgotten.

In infinity, spilled milk and dying stars matter the same.

And if you're just someone brushing your teeth late at night or you're a planet breathing your last breath as you disappear into a black hole, everything you do matters just the same. Every breath you take is as important or unimportant as the sun in the sky or the moon in the night.

Scratching your ear, is a kind of miracle, depending on how you look at it.

THE COLOURS OF STOLEN SLEEP

Now I'm awake and you're here.

Now I'm dreaming and you're here.

Now I have nothing but days.

Never nights.

THE WORLD WOULD BE EASIER

The world would be easier if the homeless were all just lazy and all they needed to do was just get a fucking job.

The world would be easier if evil were a real thing, instead of just confusion, misunderstanding, miscommunication and misplaced desire.

The world would be easier if you could just be happy for what you had, while you had it. If you could eat memories like flowers to keep your heart alive.

The world would be easier if comfort didn't rest on the backs of the broken, if your swimming pool was dug by soft hands that never worked a day in their life.

The world would be easier if we all just got rich and famous and we were all each other's #1 fan.

The world would be easier if it were an automatic.

The world would be easier.

But it isn't.

The world is hard because it requires real human effort to make it turn.

The world is hard because you may wake up today but not tomorrow. And yet no one will accept "fear of death and a futile existence" as a reasonable excuse to miss work.

The world is hard because you will have to fight for the things you love or worse, fight the things you love.

The world is hard because the things you love will kill you.

The world is hard because it was made that way by thousands upon thousands of hard men and no one wants to admit we have no idea why we're doing the things we're doing anymore.

The world is hard because it's hard to forgive and even harder to forget.

The world is hard and you should just give up, right now. Just lay down and die. Nothing will ever be easier.

But, you don't.

THE NIGHT HOLDS THE DAY SO SOFTLY

You own this hand now.

Because when I close my hand around your hand, I can feel your hand, feeling mine. And it feels the same.

THE SUN LEAVES THE EARTH

I am so selfish, so greedy and so spoiled.

How can I ask for one more day with you, when I've already had so many?

THE BANDAGES ARE MADE OF SHADOWS

You and I both know, the dark doesn't make
the bruises disappear.

It just makes them harder to see.

THE WAITING CHAIR

If it hurts you, if not being who you want to be kills you inside, just close your eyes and remember,

"Somewhere else, I'm something else.

Somewhere else, I'm something else."

And soon you will be here.

Soon, you will be you.

THE LANGUAGE STRIPPED NAKED

And I'm sorry I ever learned any words that make you cry.

I'm still doing my best to learn the ones that make you smile.

THE DARK WORDS YOU WALK DOWN AT NIGHT

This is why it hurts the way it hurts.

You have too many words in your head. There are too many ways to describe the way you feel. You will never have the luxury of a dull ache.

You must suffer through the intricacy of feeling too much.

THE MAP OF IMPERFECTIONS

I am a record of things I was born with.

These scars are my documentation of the mistakes I've made in trying to overcome them.

I am both the things I've done to myself and the things done to me.

Along these nerve endings, you will find a history of me.

THE SHIP MADE OF BROKEN PARTS CAN STILL GO ANYWHERE

You only fix the things you feel deserve to be fixed, as if you're a special kind of person who doesn't deserve to sort their own life out because of who they are. Like your brokenness is a symptom of being you.

"I can let that wait, I don't need to do this because I don't deserve to have it done. My life is always only ever incomplete."

And yet, no one deserves the full benefit of being you, more than you.

THE PAST KEEPS GOING AWAY

After you're gone, people will forget your name, no matter how important it was, and your face, no matter how pretty it was, and what you said, no matter how clever any of it sounded.

The things you've done will crumble and fade and the places you once loved, will change and be given new names.

You are only here for one moment and it lasts exactly one lifetime.

THE CHILD WITH THE INVISIBLE HEAD

And what still shocks me, is how often the thing that hurts you, looks like the thing that helps you.

THE SAD SEA WAVES

When I look at you, I can see the person you used to be drowning in the person you are. And it makes me nostalgic and sad because I know when you look at me, you must see the same thing.

THE PEACE I WON WHEN I STOPPED FIGHTING

I'm sorry, but no gun can frighten me and no word can hurt me. No wave can knock me over and no rain can slow me. No night can tire me and no fire can burn me.

Because I have found the strength to do the things I believe in, and the will to stop doing the things I don't believe in.

So I have discovered what it means, to be at peace.

And you, my friend, will never find a big enough gun.

THE HEART CAN NOT BE DISCOUNTED

If they put you back on the shelf, in exchange for someone else, don't worry.

Someone better's coming along.

THE REASON THEY DON'T LISTEN

There's no beauty in your truth because
there's no truth in your beauty.

THE LIMITED OPPORTUNITY

There are only so many of us born at a time and we are thrown into the world to find each other, to find the other ones who don't think you're strange, who understand your jokes, your smile, the way you talk.

There are only so many of us born at a time and we only have so long to find each other before we die.

But we have to try.

THE LAST LAND I STOOD ON

And my fingers are ships
sailing on your skin,
slowly drifting and hoping
against hope that they fall off
the edge of the earth.

And your heart is nothing
but the gravity pulling me
towards you.

THE FIRST DAY ON EARTH

First, you need to relax. I know it's not as warm as it once was but you get used to the cold and warmth can be found in the people around you. Secondly, do not get used to crying to get things. Some people never grow out of it. Avoid them. Spend time around people who smile in the face of despair. Learn from them all you can. Everyone is a lesson. A story. A unique and wondrous perspective on the chaos that is human existence. The more people you talk to, the more you understand it. But never speak if you have the opportunity to listen. Especially if you want someone to like you. There's nothing you can say that'll endear someone to you as much as really and truly listening to them. You are on day one of a sometimes remarkable, sometimes terrible, sometimes beautiful, strange and always completely unknown journey. Be ok with this. Worrying about what happens next will ruin the surprise. You will meet strange people along the way, some good, some bad. This is a pattern that will more than likely repeat constantly as you grow up. Some things will be good, some things will be bad. Neither will ever last forever. Nothing will stay the same. Appreciate every moment of happiness and remember it when you despair. Hold them close. And when you are happy, remember the moments of despair and think to yourself, "I told you so." Never let someone else define you. You are your own creation and only you decide how you feel, who you are and what you want. This can be scary at first but it is liberating to truly and utterly embrace your own identity. People who hate you for not being like them are not worth hating back. Please, let go of hate whenever you can. Accept love whenever it is given and give it out freely. It is the most powerful force on earth.

Enjoy your stay.

THE PURPOSE OF LOVE

When I don't know how I'm supposed to feel, you're the only person that can remind me.

THE DEARLY DISCARDED

Late at night, when your brain is tired of thinking of everything else, you will find me there. You cannot throw me far enough away.

THE TRAIN HIT ME AND I DIDN'T FEEL IT

You shouldn't fall asleep on your heart. It'll go numb.

THE DESIRE TO LIVE UNDERWATER FOREVER

If I breathe you in and you breathe me out, I swear we can breathe forever. I swear I'll find summer in your winter and spring in your autumn and always, hands at the ends of your fingers, arms at the ends of your shoulders and I swear, when we run out of forever, when we run out of air, your name will be the last word that my lungs make air for.

THE ENDLESS PUNCHLINE

Great, real, true love should feel like an inside joke that only you and them can laugh at.

No matter what the world does to either of you.

THE FOOTSTEPS MADE OF FIRE

When you bring light, be careful of those who cannot see,
who would try to bring you dark.

THE THINGS WHICH AREN'T LOVE

Your salary is not love and your word is not love. Your clothes are not love and holding hands is not love. Sex is not love and a kiss is not love. Long letters are not love and a text is not love. Flowers are not love and a box of chocolates is not love. Sunsets are not love and photographs are not love. The stars are not love and a beach under the moonlight is not love. The smell of someone else on your pillow is not love and the feeling of their skin touching your skin is not love. Heart-shaped candy is not love and an overseas holiday is not love. The truth is not love and winning an argument is not love. Warm coffee isn't love and cheap cards bought from stores are not love. Tears are not love and laughter is not love. A head on a shoulder is not love and messages written at the front of books given as gifts are not love. Apathy is not love and numbness is not love. A pain in your chest is not love and clenching your fist is not love. Rain is not love.

Only you. Only you, are love.

THE DAYS BEFORE CHILDHOOD

Before now, before you're here, we're getting the world ready. We've softened all the corners. We've taken all the chemicals out of everything we've ever made and used them to make fireworks to mark your arrival. We've invented leaves that fall 20% slower and are 100% more fun to fall into. We made new colours. We made snow. We made summer holidays. We've even created something called a "puppy" and a "kitten" and you may choose which one you prefer when you get here. Which is where we are now.

Before you are born.

THE WAVES PUT YOU TO SLEEP

I love you like I love the sea. And I'm ok with drowning.

THE ECHO INSPECTOR

"Why am I still here?"

"You're not. You're a ghost."

"I thought I left."

"You did. You're always leaving."

"Where am I now?"

"Always here. Never here again."

THE GRAND DISTRACTION

And every day, the world will drag you by the hand, yelling, "This is important! And this is important! And this is important! You need to worry about this! And this! And this!"

And each day, it's up to you, to yank your hand back, put it on your heart and say, "No. This is what's important."

THE CLEAREST LENS

And may you never wish that life would pass with background music in a black and white montage. And may you lust and hunger for every awkward second of real life, in all it's un-retouched glory.

THE TRUTH AS IT CURRENTLY STANDS

You will not remember much from school.

School is designed to teach you how to respond and listen to authority figures in the event of an emergency. Like if there's a bomb in a mall or a fire in an office. It can, apparently, take you more than a decade to learn this. These are not the best days of your life. They are still ahead of you. You will fall in love and have your heart broken in many different, new and interesting ways in college or university (if you go) and you will actually learn things, as at this point, people will believe you have a good chance of obeying authority and surviving, in the event of an emergency. If, in your chosen career path, there are award shows that give out more than ten awards in one night or you have to pay someone to actually take the award home to put on your mantlepiece, then those awards are more than likely designed to make young people in their 20's work very late, for free, for other people. Those people will do their best to convince you that they have value. They don't. Only the things you do have real, lasting value, not the things you get for the things you do. You will, at some point, realise that no trophy loves you as much as you love it, that it cannot pay your bills (even if it increases your salary slightly) and that it won't hold your hand tightly as you say your last words on your deathbed. Only people who love you can do that. If you make art to feel better, make sure it eventually makes you feel better. If it doesn't, stop making it. You will love someone differently, as time passes. If you always expect to feel the same kind of love you felt when you first met someone, you will always be looking for new people to love. Love doesn't fade. It just changes as it grows. It would be boring if it didn't. There is no truly "right" way of writing, painting, being or thinking, only things which have happened before. People who tell you differently are assholes, petrified of change, who should be violently ignored. No philosophy, mantra or piece of advice will hold true for every conceivable situation. "The early bird catches the worm" does not apply to minefields. Perfection only exists in poetry and movies, everyone fights occasionally and no sane person is ever completely sure of anything. Nothing is wrong with any of this. Wisdom does not come from age, wisdom comes from doing things. Be very, very careful of people who call themselves wise, artists, poets or gurus. If you eat well, exercise often and drink enough water, you have a good chance of living a long and happy life. The only time you can really be happy, is right now. There is no other moment that exists that is more important than this one. Do not sacrifice this moment in the hopes of a better one. It is easy to remember all these things when they are being said, it is much harder to remember them when you are stuck in traffic or lying in bed worrying about the next day. If you want to move people, simply tell them the truth. Today, it is rarer than it's ever been.

THE TREES GROW QUIETLY

The things you struggle with today are things you choose to struggle with.

Because you believe that what you want to accomplish, is worth struggling for.

THE ENDLESS NIGHT AND ALL IT PROMISES

You can be beautiful and new forever. Give me forever and I'll prove it.

THE PAIN UNFELT

I have told myself you are not allowed to hurt me anymore.
That's what hurts the most.

THE SPACE BETWEEN OXYGEN AND HYDROGEN

When the air touches water, it makes a mirror. When I touch you, you do the same.

THE NOISE AND COLOUR

When you make eye contact, break it immediately. Check the time repeatedly. Because it's easiest to be alone in a crowd. And I am more alone in a crowd, than I ever am on my own.

THE REASON FOR AIRPORTS

You can only hurt someone until there's
nothing left to hurt.

THE REMAINING MIRRORS

And I hide because there's more to me than what you see and I'm not sure you'd like the rest. I know that sometimes, I don't like the rest.

THE GLASS ATTIC OF MY MIND

What would you like to tell yourself today, to make yourself feel ok?

THE LINE BETWEEN MADNESS AND LIFE

When I'm crazy, you tell me it's just the chemicals in my brains mixing and unmixing themselves at the wrong time.

When I'm in love, you tell me it's as real as sunshine and we're greater than just molecules and air.

So I choose to believe different things, depending on my love. Depending on my chemicals. At the time.

THE HOUSE WE KEEP MOMENTS IN

May you do the things you want to and always remember what it felt like when you were doing them.

THE DEFIANCE OF THE DIFFERENT

Most importantly, if you can at all avoid it, don't be normal. Strive, burn and do everything you can to avoid being the industry standard. Even the highest industry standard. Be greater than anything anyone else has ever dreamed of you. Don't settle for pats on the back, salary increases, a nod-and-a-smile. Instead, rage against the tepidness of the mundane with every fiber of whatever makes you, you. Change this place.

Please, do that for me.

THE REMAINING ME

Even after the entire world
has taken me apart, there's
still a part of me left for you.

THE CARRINGTON EVENT

Love proudly. Let it burn anything between you.

THE DAY WE STOPPED DYING

You're wrong.
The question is not,
"How many times can your heart be broken?"
 The question is,
"How many times can it heal?"

THE MIDDLE OF THE UNIVERSE

I understand that you care. I just sometimes feel that the people who know me best, are people I've never met.

THE PAIN OF EACH OTHER

I do not understand why you would go out of your way to hurt each other, when life can already hurt so much.

THE WORLD OF YOUR OWN

How sad it is to be somewhere else, when you're here.

THE ENVY OF A BILLION LITTLE UNIQUE SNOWFLAKES

I don't care what people think. I fell in love with you. Not people.

THE ORDER IN WHICH THINGS ARE DRAWN

No picture of a person ever feels alive until you draw in the eyes.
So open your eyes. Let at least one of us feel alive.

THE SALTING OF THE EARTH

You should know that there is something worse than hate and that is unlove.

Because hate is anger over something lost, hate is passion, hate is misguided, it's caring for the wrong things but it is still caring.

But unlove, unlove is to unkiss, to unremember, to unhold, to undream, to undo everything that ever was and leave smooth stone behind in its wake.

No fire.

No fury.

Just, nothing.

And that is worse than hate.

THE HIDDEN DEPTHS

You've got to keep looking for them, even after you find them.
Otherwise, you lose them.

THE AIR CARRIES YOU AWAY

I've tried to put you down on paper so many times.

But you keep getting up.

THE LIGHT OF FUTURE MEMORIES

You make me nostalgic for a love that hasn't even happened yet.

THE VOICE IN THE BACK OF MY HEART

When you have nothing left to say to me, say it anyway.

THE DIFFERENT WAYS I DIE

And it made me lay awake, thinking of everyone I've ever known who died.

And I hoped that someone would lay awake one night, thinking of me.

(Don't worry. I will feel enough for all of you.)

THE EVENTUAL GHOST

You have until the hour you die to do everything you've ever really wanted to do and say everything you've ever really wanted to say. It sounds less fair when you get older.

THE AGE AT WHICH IT HAPPENS

One day, you realise that there are some people you'll never see again. At least, not in the same way.

THE WAY HOME

If photographs of you are as close as I can get, then that's as close as I'll get.

If the edge of the land, is as close as I can get, then that's as close as I'll get.

If right up beside you is as close as I can get, then that's as close as I'll get.

I have and always will be, as close as I can get.

THE IMPORTANCE OF BREAKING THINGS AND PEOPLE

Just so you know, there are certain people who were put here to break you.

So you could learn how to pull yourself back together again.

THE STRANGEST DAYS

And when I'm far from home and I feel like an alien, trust me, somehow I never left you.

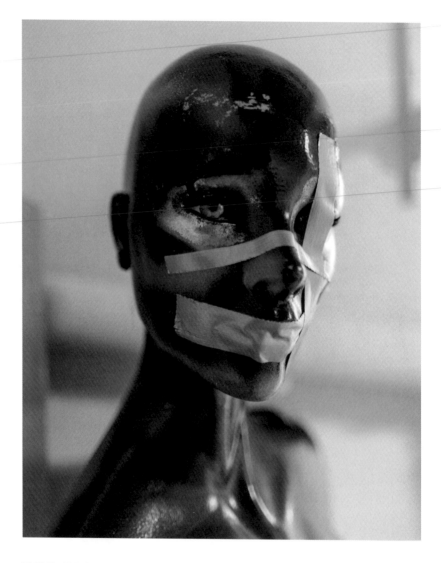

THE TRUTH IS DIFFERENT EVERY DAY

You keep trying to tell the truth about who you are but you keep changing, every time someone listens.

THE BEAUTIFUL TRAP

If you open up too much, people can fall in and hurt themselves.

THE WORDS ARE ALL IN LANGUAGES I DO NOT SPEAK

And yet, when you get here, you are not given instructions. No one tells you that heart A is meant to slot into heart B. There are no diagrams about how you are meant to live each day or directions on how to assemble some semblance of happiness. You are not even told what colours to paint your feelings or, given a purpose and a reason for your life.

You have to make all of it up. You have to make all of it, yourself.

THE BROKEN ICE IN YOUR WAKE

I have a list in my head of all the feelings I still want to feel before I die. And you have ticked so many things off that list.

THE DIFFERENCES BETWEEN US ARE THE SAME

If you're like me, then I know you're trying. And I want you to know that if I ever stop, I'd want you to carry on.

THE RELATIVE PHENOMENA

I would do my taxes. Fill out insurance forms.

Count grains of rice in a bag.

Whatever made time pass the slowest with you.

THE STANDARD OPERATING PROCEDURES

No matter how hard you try, you will never be stranger than what the world considers normal.

THE THINGS WE ARE SUPPOSED TO BE

Just so you know, I don't. And I refuse to care.

THE GRINNING FOOL

Each night, somewhere out there, people go to bed, petrified that I might be happy as I am.

And I wake up each day and make their worst fears come true.

P.S.

I hope you're happy.

THE VIOLENT PEACE

You kill death every day that you live.

And I do my best to murder hate whenever I have the chance to love.

THE DAY YOU SHOT ME IN THE BACK OF THE HEAD

The sun rose like it does on any other day, on the day you shot me in the back of the head.

I'd just made coffee and you'd come back from doing the groceries and I asked if you wanted some without turning my head to look at you, on the day you shot me in the back of the head.

And I hit the floor so slowly and so hard and without any real warning, on the day you shot me in the back of the head.

I knew we'd had our differences and our silences but I didn't expect it to end like this, on the day you shot me in the back of the head.

I thought there'd be more time, on the day you shot me in the back of the head.

If I was still alive at that point, I imagine I'd smell cordite and sulphur filling the room and hear the echoes bouncing off the walls, on the day you shot me in the back of the head.

I imagine there was a look of surprise on my face, on the day you shot me in the back of the head.

I wonder if you thought you were being merciful by waiting until I wasn't looking, on the day you shot me in the back of the head.

I probably stared off at a distant point, while you gathered your things together and left, on the day you shot me in the back of the head.

And I know that my body was there for a while and that the room was dark and that it was very quiet, because of what you'd done, on the day you shot me in the back of the head.

But what you might not know, is that I got up.

And washed my face.

And the sun rose again.

On the day after you shot me in the back of the head.

THE STUFF AND THE THINGS

If you like a whole bunch of things and I like a whole bunch of things, maybe one of the things that we both like, can be each other.

THE SHOT STARS

If your star falls down, you will find mine lying beside yours.

THE THINGS I MEANT

A heart was meant to beat. And air was meant to be breathed, close to your ear. And your skin was meant to remember what mine felt like. And some songs were meant to play on repeat. And the sun was meant to come down. And we were meant to ignore it when it woke up. And days were meant to pass. And nights were meant to follow. And your eyes were meant to cry out whatever pain was left.

And I never meant to hurt you.

But I guess that's what everyone says.

THE LONGEST SHADOW

You know what I would do for love. But no one ever asked me how
far I would go, for loss.

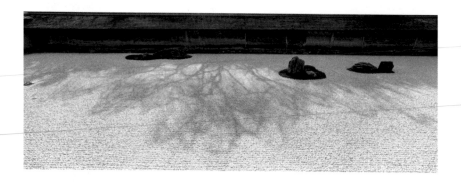

THE BILLIONS OF PIECES

The human heart is made from the only substance in the universe that can become stronger, after it's been broken.

THE SIMILARITIES DIDN'T MAKE US THE SAME

You spend your whole life learning what you shouldn't care about.
Until one day you find out you didn't care enough.

THE DEFECT AT THE HEART FACTORY

There is no heart you can have that another heart will not have a problem with.

THE SUN WILL FREEZE BEFORE I DO

I promised a lot.

But never that I wouldn't get back up after you knocked me down.

Never that my broken remains wouldn't catch fire.

Never that I wouldn't burn through the ice and snow one more time.

And you can slam your glaciers into to me, so slowly, and even though they hurt, I will not go numb from the cold, I will not pass out from the pain, I will look up at you and the world and whisper through bloody teeth,

"More..."

THE LIGHT FROM FROZEN GRAVES

"But I just want to stop feeling."

"As far as I can tell, there's only one way to stop feeling and that's to die."

"That seems a bit drastic."

"It is drastic. Perhaps the most drastic thing there is. There are other ways to kill feelings, like drinking a lot or working hard, constantly, pushing those around you as far away as possible until there's no way for you to reach out to them but ultimately, the only way to completely stop feeling, forever, is to die."

"I'm not sure I'm ready for that."

"Good. You'll be a better person for it."

"What do you mean?"

"I mean that the most interesting, amazing people I've ever met, the ones who influenced and shaped the universe itself, are the ones that felt too much but lived through it."

"That sounds hard."

"It is. It involves living."

THE STORM BEFORE THE CALM

You're still here but I am still the sea. And as peaceful as I seem, please don't ever turn your back on me.

THE THINGS I HAVE FELT HAVE TORN ME APART

Those who walk away from you in the dark should be forgotten in the light.

THE PHANTOM LIMBS

And when we speak now, seldom as that is, the old language returns. I wonder if it makes old names make guest appearances in your mind. If you can feel the skin of my neck near yours one more time. Do you reach across the bed for a shape, no longer there. Do you remember it clearly or is it all just memories of memories. Is there still warmth from my fingers tracing the contours of your skin, left somewhere in your body. If you smell the smell of how I used to smell in a crowd, do you think of these things. Is something missing in everyone else's or someone new's voice. Will they never know quite how to laugh or breathe just behind your ear. Do they know what you look like when you want to leave a party, when you've had too much of people. Could they rebuild your body out of clay if they needed to, because they've touched it so many times. Does your back still arch the way it used to when I still kissed you.

Does an old singer sing an old song on an old radio.

Do the lyrics still shake your fucking soul.

Did it sound like this?

THE EXPANDING DISTANCE BETWEEN TWO POINTS

Making you regret what you did to me is not 'me winning'.

It's everyone still losing.

THE UNIVERSE WILL TAKE YOU

They might not like you at school.

And they might not like you at work.

And they might not like you in a park.

And they might not like you on the moon.

And they might not like you in summer.

When you say they remind you of winter.

But this universe, will always love you.

This universe, will take you.

THE MISSING BREAD CRUMBS

Stop telling me to follow my heart. It once led me to you.

THE MORNING BELL

"Did you see them? With all their feelings hanging out? With their emotions exposed?"

"I know, what a freak."

"What are you doing tonight?"

"Crying myself to sleep, wondering why I never truly feel loved. You?"

"Same."

THE FINAL EXAM

a) Rain is the sound of the night rolling over in its sleep.

b) Rain is a record of broken promises and each one is sent back to earth to clean it.

c) Rain is life by a 1000 cuts.

d) Rain is a coronary anesthetic.

e) Rain is the world secretly crying for you, when no one else will.

THE DIFFERENT KINDS OF SILENCE

There's a silence you can only find after a phone has been put down in anger, another one that only exists for a moment after a door is slammed.

But there is also a silence that a smile makes when you smile it and a silence that loves makes, when you love it.

THE START OF THE WORLD WIDE WAR

Please know that they shot first, when they tried to outlaw our entire culture and our way of being, when they threw us off our land.

Please understand that our only weapons were our eyes and our collective voices and when they marched on us, when they raised their clubs in rude salutes to the sun, we held up our camera phones and said over and over and over again:

The whole world is watching.

The whole world is watching.

The whole world is watching.

And when they were so ashamed of who they were, they wanted, needed us to close our eyes, they pepper-sprayed our faces, as we held each other close, as they revealed their true nature, to the tune of 1000, 1000 jackboots marching and we sat there and cried.

Please know that they did their best to divide us, to tell us that where the water met the dirt we were born on was somehow sacred, that the strips of colour on the flap of fabric waving above our heads were holy, that the way the light refracted off our skins defined our character.

They drove their cars through us in Tahir Square and they took our pensions on Wall Street and then they told us we were going to jail because we shared songs with each other.

I know that you do not have fat, bloated middlemen, I know the dictators have fallen, I know that the gatekeepers have all faded out and you live as earthlings, undivided by imaginary borders and differences.

Because I know I was born here on the blue electric fields, in the democracy of ideas, in the new country.

And this is a place worth dying for.

THE GAP BETWEEN WHO YOU ARE AND WHO YOU WANT TO BE

Nothing can be beautiful.

Not all the spaces inside you need to be filled.

Who you still have the chance to be, lives in the spaces you give yourself.

THE CORRECT AND PROPER WAY TO FEEL

"Is this how I'm supposed to feel now?"

"I don't know, I'll check the manual."

"And?"

"It says that you're feeling the right way."

"What way is that?"

"It says that there is no right way to feel but, right now, after something like this happens, you do need to feel however you're feeling and that feeling this way, however you're feeling, is healthy."

"That doesn't sound very scientific."

"It has nothing to do with science."

"Does it say anything else?"

"It says you'll break something if you beat yourself up for the way you feel and that you won't be able to feel differently until you've finished feeling this feeling."

"Ok. How long will that take?"

"I don't know. How do you feel?"

THE LANGUAGE OF STARS

Love:

To discover there's at least one other real person on planet Earth.

Loss:

To discover that the aliens, can look just like you.

THE SNOW FALLS ON FOREVER (HUSH)

You can't miss forever.

No matter how close forever feels right now.

You can't hurt forever.

Even if your heart whispers in your ear and tries to convince you otherwise.

You can't bleed forever.

Sooner or later, you will either die or live.

Neither of us can do anything for forever.

Because forever passed away, long ago.

THE HATE FEEDS THE HATE

You say there is an 'us' and a 'them' and we must fight.

I say there is only an us. And we must love.

THE WAR AGAINST THE SEA

You say that only a fool believes that everyone has some good in their heart.

You say that only a fool makes music in their mind.

You say that only a fool loves hate back.

You say that only a fool leans against the wind.

You say that only a fool takes on a planet.

You say that only a fool holds out hope.

You say that only a fool tries to fly.

You say that only a fool fights the sea.

Very well.

I am that fool. And I will die fighting.

THE STATE OF THE ARTIST

You, as an artist, have the greatest responsibility of all.

You are charged with trying to make people feel, in a world that tells them not to.

You are tasked with speaking soft words, painting, playing, filming, writing moments of such magnitude and beauty that people rediscover their hearts one more (last) time.

You are here to give meaning to the few decades we spend here.

That is the reason you were sent to Earth.

THE FRACTALS OF TIME PASSING

Today you became a yesterday, when once you were a tomorrow.

THE BREAKING OF PEOPLE

You can try being broken and you can try forgetting. All I know is I am no longer broken about the things I have forgotten.

THE WORLD IS A MONSTER

Scratching at the windows
and the door, the world
could not wait to kill us.

They got in so slowly, with
distractions and memos,
with forgotten dinners
and missed calls.

No.

The world could not wait
to kill us.

And I clutched you close,
and I swear: I wished on
every wish, that neither of
us would fall.

But, no.

The world could not wait
to kill us.

And we died.

THE FEELING OF SOMEONE DRAWING YOU

And if you want to know the feeling I'm talking about, run your own fingers slowly through your hair, and pretend they're someone else's.

THE WORLD CHANGED, NOT ME

You think I'm unreasonable.

But in an unreasonable world, that's just how I look.

THE LAST PART OF THIS SENTENCE IS STILL YOURS

You still take things from me in the most beautiful way.

You are still the only way I can sleep, when I wake up to tell you, I cannot sleep.

You still make sense in a way that only birds know when they leave winter.

THE QUIET REBELLION

Challenge the world that gives you the chance to live longer but asks you to do small things with that longer life.

THE WORDS I WILL READ SO WE RECOGNISE EACH OTHER WHEN WE MEET AGAIN

Don't get me wrong, I'm happy, happier than I've probably ever been. If you detect any sadness, it is only because I have found you in this life but I am not sure if I have found you in previous lives and I am worried about finding you in future ones.

What if there is a series of sad me's going backwards and forwards in time who did not and do not find you?

What if this is the only point of light along that infinite line?

So I am sorry if there is a hint of sadness.

I am just feeling sorry for myself.

THE ALCHEMY MACHINE

If you can take the sadness and despair the world gives you and breathe it back out as love and hope, breathe some back to me.

THE FIRE IN THE STREETS

Between the fire and you and your skin, there is no room for light.

And the rocks that survived the heat around me only weighed me down.

But I still put a rock inside my heart so I can remember what it felt like to swim up, from the bottom of a volcano.

THE MEMORY OF BEAUTY

I hope things are beautiful. And if they're not, then I hope you remember this moment right now when they are. Because you've got to hold up each and every other moment to the moment when things are beautiful and say,

"Look. I told you. Remember this."

THE DESCENT INTO LIGHT

If you're not afraid, there is no end, only an imminent bliss. So burn like love and love like fire.

THE SAME RIVER, TWICE

Everyone changes so slowly, they don't even know that they have.

And everyone likes to pretend that things are just the same yet they look at you like you could bring something back that's supposed to already be here.

But home is a time. Not just a place.

THE FATE OF THOSE BORN IN DIRT

When I end, I will end as a tree ends: as a fire, bleeding out the sunlight from every summer it lived.

So do not judge me yet.

You have only seen, how I begin.

THE LIGHT THAT SHINES WHEN THINGS END

I hope that in the future they invent a small golden light that follows you everywhere and when something is about to end, it shines brightly so you know it's about to end.

And if you're never going to see someone again, it'll shine brightly and both of you can be polite and say, "It was nice to have you in my life while I did, good luck with everything that happens after now."

And maybe if you're never going to eat at the same restaurant again, it'll shine and you can order everything off the menu you've never tried. Maybe, if someone's about to buy your car, the light will shine and you can take it for one last spin.

Maybe, if you're with a group of friends who'll never be together again, all your lights will shine at the same time and you'll know, and then you can hold each other and whisper,

"This was so good. Oh my God, this was so good."

THE INFINITE DISTANCE

Your poetry is lonely. And yet, you write to feel less alone.

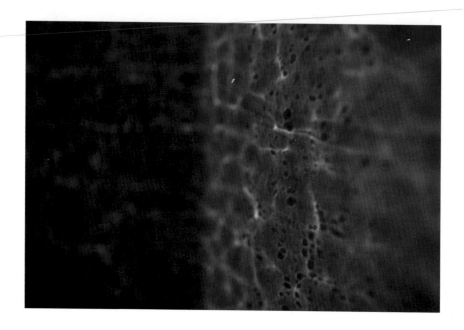